YOUR BIGGER FUTURE

How To Start Turning Your Dreams Into Reality By Utilizing DreamNumber™

By Kort R. McCulley

Copyright © 2014 Kort R. McCulley
All rights reserved.

Cover Design & Book Layout By Bethany Weber Design

Printed In the United States Of America

ISBN-10: 1503088820
ISBN-13: 978-1503088825

Testimonials

"Whether you're dreaming big or dreaming small success can only be achieved through an executable plan. Kort's knowledge, integrity, passion and trust has allowed me to start dreaming again and turn them into a reality!"

Steve Lanci, Enterprise Sales at CDW

"Kort's passion is making big dreams come true and is an extraordinary resource to tap into when you need to create your own dreams!"

Eric "Pete" Kingdon, Senior Audit Manager at BMO Harris

"As consumers seek a more significant connected experience and as their dreams continue to get bigger and bigger, so does their search for a process and a platform to help make it all possible. This book addresses the needed structure in a few short and effective steps."

Tony DiLeonardi, Author Of "Face To Face: Creating Lifelong & Multigenerational Clients"

"This book outlines the impossible dreams and makes them come to life with unrelenting commitment and structure that takes shape right away. "

Jason Nash, President Of Assisted Care At Home

"In Your Bigger Future, Kort first and foremost give you permission to think big... to dream. In today's hectic world, a world of uncertainty, it's too easy to get sucked into believing we need to play it safe. Kort provides the inspiration and lays out the steps to dream the dream again leading you to a bigger future and fulfilling life."

Dirk Beveridge, Founder UnleashWD

A Special Thank You

This book would not have been possible without my coaches and support team at the Strategic Coach, Susan Austin's navigation of this book and the team at 90MinuteBook.com and Adrienne Rubio.

Paul and Rochelle Petefish, Matt Lesh, Susan Moore, Eric Hobbs, Tom Korder, Steve and Katie Lanci, Eric "Pete" Kingdon, Jason and Victoria Nash, Tony DiLeonardi, Chris and Katie Borth, and the list goes on of those who graciously shared their stories that shaped the book. Thank you all for making an impact in my life and helping me make this dream a reality!

And, most importantly, to my family, friends, and clients that generated the initial inspiration to get this project in motion. It's your stories that pushed me to educate the world on how to live your dreams every day! My Grandfather was a big time dreamer and I plan to carry that on with the rest of the world!

"All successful people, men and women, are big dreamers. They imagine what their future could be, ideal in every respect, and then they work every day toward their distant vision, that goal or purpose."

Brian Tracy

Here's What's Inside…

9 Introduction

15 Your Bigger Future!

21 Why Don't More People Dream?

31 How Dreams Can Change Your View of What Is Possible…

39 How to Use Dreams to Create Your Bigger Future…

49 Don't Focus on Goals, Focus on Dreams…

55 Why You Should Dream Big!

67 Why You Should Never Stop Dreaming…

71 Here's How the DreamNumber ™ Online Application Works…

89 Here's Exactly How to Get Started on Your Bigger Future Today…

"You can live your dreams if you can embrace change. It's by taking chances that you'll learn how to be brave."

Nikita Koloff

Introduction

Your Bigger Future | Westchester, IL | November 2014

My vision of dreaming starts with my late grandfather, John, he was forced to drop out of school in the 8th grade to help feed his family of eight (six brothers and his father) during the Great Depression. One day after milking the cows they were taking the cream to town as the source of income for the week's food.

While he and his brothers were playing around they knocked over the entire can of cream. As they looked at their father expecting to be reprimanded for their horseplay, they found him in tears uncertain about how he was going to feed the family for the week. They banked on that cream to carry them through the week and it was gone in an instant. It was these events early in his life that drove him to build a stable lifestyle for his family; no horseplay until the cream gets to town.

From that humble beginning he went on to chase his dream of becoming a successful entrepreneur far from the fight of feeding his family. What started as a small business in a garage selling feed and grain to farmers is now one of the largest pork producers in the nation. Grandpa John has since passed this thriving business down to his sons (Bob, Mark, and John Jr.) and fellow employees but his legacy and dreams still live on. I have gained a ton of inspiration over the years from my grandfather and my Dad in watching the development of some big dreams take shape. Regardless of where you begin, what I have seen firsthand leads me to believe that any dream is possible.

One of the things I get asked a lot is why am I so passionate about dreams? You see it's been my experience that somewhere over the last generation a majority of the world stopped dreaming. My grandfather was able to achieve his dream of creating a successful multi-generational business, and I believe it was his mindset that he could do whatever he intended with his life that allowed him to quickly make this all a reality and never stop working towards the next set of dreams. Spending time with my grandfather helped pass these beliefs onto me and it has now become my passion to pass them onto others as well.

I've been sharing my passion for dreaming big with my clients for years. And because they are creating big dreams they are creating big results. I believe no matter where you are in your life, if you allow yourself to put aside "I cant's" and really dream, you can change the course of your life forever…starting now.

I hope this book educates you and encourages you to start on your journey to creating Your Bigger Future. So…what are your dreams? Are you ready to start making progress on them today?

Cheers to your success!

Kort R. McCulley

"When you have a dream you've got to grab it and never let go."

Carol Burnett

Your Bigger Future!

Susan: Good afternoon. This is Susan Austin, and I'm super excited to be here with Kort McCulley. Kort's going to be sharing with us his thoughts and ideas about how to dream again. Welcome, Kort.

Kort: Hello Susan, thank you for having me today.

Susan: I'm excited about this book Kort. Let's start off with why you want to write this book?

Kort: I noticed a long time ago people, for some reason, have stopped dreaming. And because they stopped dreaming they stopped planning. Because they stopped planning, they start to feel as if they have failed in life. I believe it all starts with the lack of dreaming.

I wanted to write this book to encourage people to start dreaming again. I want people to know that they are allowed to dream! There are many formulas for success, but I believe true success starts with having a big dream. Working towards those dreams and creating a pattern of great results is a huge part of why some people are successful at achieving their bigger future. I want to give people permission to dream again.

I'm very passionate about dreaming. I started to notice people around me who were settling. Somewhere along the path they lost sight of a bigger future for themselves. They were saying, "My future is as big as what I can see and what I can see is not very far."

So they just sort of gave up and stopped dreaming. I became passionate about working with those people and giving them advice on how to tap back into that little boy or girl who used to dream.

It's what I love to do! Day after day I meet with people of all walks of life, and we have a discussion on what their future may look like. This isn't something that just happens. You have to create the space for dreaming in your life.

I ask them what they aspired to be when they came out of college or even when they went to college. Their futures probably looked pretty bright back then. They were excited about their future, but somewhere along the path their dreams faded. As a result of some of the decisions they made or some of the decisions they didn't make, they have been left in a holding pattern, not sure what to do next…far from dreaming. And when we looked at what is behind those mediocre results, I found it was because they stopped dreaming. In the position I am in, consulting for companies and their workforce on ways to arrive at a secure retirement, I've had the opportunity to meet people who are in full retirement to young professionals just beginning to start their first job or pursue their dream careers. Over time, I got really passionate about the different worlds each of these individuals were in.

Take two people who could be complete opposites yet they share the similarity of dreaming. Some started dreaming early and continued to do it their entire life, and their future became much bigger. Then there are those who didn't dream at all, where did they end up? Going back to those who are young with the opportunity to still influence their future outcomes before life's complexities set in, they need to know that they should keep dreaming to create the bigger future they desire. They are fresh into the working world, and for the first time they can achieve greatness. They need to know how to create a plan, how to execute their plan, and how to change their world into something great. They are at the beginning of creating a fulfilled life! That's what got me passionate. Because when they dream big and create a plan, they will create a much bigger future for themselves!

Susan: You're like the dream whisperer. We need more of this.

Kort: I never thought of it like that. However, our purpose is to be a **Dream Consultant** to our clients and help them make their dreams a reality! That's what we do every day.

" Every great dream begins with a dreamer. Always remember, you have within you the strength, the patience, and the passion to reach for the stars to change the world."

Harriet Tubman

Why Don't More People Dream?

Susan: Why do you think people have stopped dreaming Kort?

Kort: I believe there are lots of reasons people stop dreaming. It might not always be socially acceptable to admit your big dreams. "You're dreaming so big, John. You think you're really going to accomplish that?"

Friends, perhaps family, who have lost their ability to dream, may look at you and say, "I really don't know if I want you to do bigger and better than I did because how will that make me look?" Social pressure to remain in the status quo is very real. For their own self-preservation, and often they don't even know they are doing this, they will try and talk you out of it, and all under the guise of 'this is for your own good.' "That's a big dream. What happens if you try it and fail? Then where will you be?" Or, "I don't know, John. It seems to me there is a lot of risk in going for it." **The pressure from family and society to not rock the boat is a big reason people stop dreaming.**

For some people, it might be they don't have the confidence or clarity about what it's going to take in order to make their dream possible. For some, they didn't have anybody to encourage them to dream when growing up. They didn't have a support group or trusted mentor. They lacked the motivation, discipline, advice, and/or didn't have the proper tools and resources.

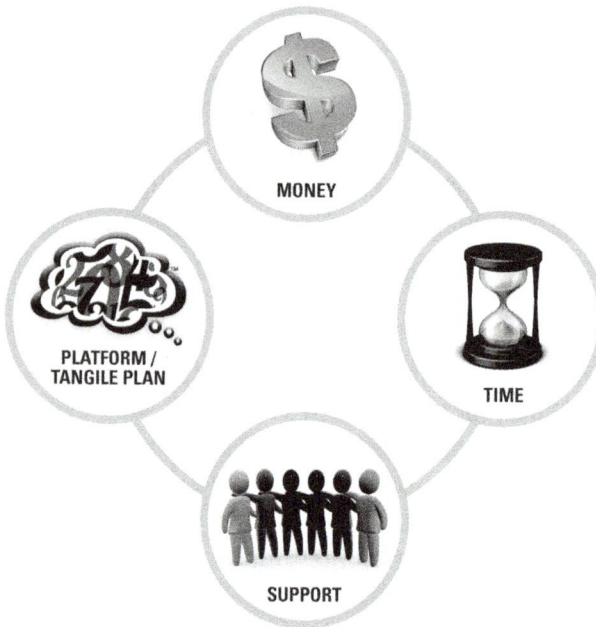

Another obstacle is they couldn't figure out how to gather the money to accomplish their goal. So they talk themselves out of it before they get started. "I can't do this without money." They don't know how to solve life's equations to get the money needed to accomplish their dreams.

I believe a lot of times they lose focus. Let's face it; our lives are busier than ever. They don't have a way to ensure their dreams don't get pushed to the back burner. They just don't know how to go back and revisit their dreams and keep track of the progress on them to make sure that they're on track to make it a reality.

"All these other things I have going on in my life, and suddenly the trip I always wanted to take to Hawaii looks somewhat unreasonable. I want to go to Hawaii, and I have three young children. I can't go on vacation with three children. Who's going to take care of the kids? Have you seen the price of airfares lately? UGH!"

With life going at the speed it does nowadays, it's easy for someone to let obstacles take the place of their dreams and that will eliminate the dreams from actually becoming a reality. Suddenly, they find themselves in a new position in life with new responsibilities, and they never get out of it. Suddenly they are towards the end of the game, they're in retirement, and they look around and ask themselves, "Have I done all the things I wanted to do at this point in my life?" Very often the answer is "No. No, I haven't." Why? What got in the way of your dreams?

I think you would be overwhelmed with the feedback we get from people. They tell us, "I got to this point, and I never would have thought I wouldn't have gone to Hawaii." Why? What got into the way of that dream? Some people admit to missing out on some of their dreams, and some people will say, "Oh, I've done everything I thought I would do." Really? Show me the dreams you have completed.

We have this young couple that is the perfect example of achieving their dream...now! Paul and Rochelle love to travel and their passion for traveling is a major piece to their relationship. Together they have traveled to 12 countries and counting in just 10 years! Their dream of seeing the world is a priority and they plan for it to remain a priority in the future. These two are in a constant cycle of planning, saving and traveling. It's inspiring and they make their dreams happen!

But the reality is they have lost sight of their dreams. When they were younger, I bet they thought they were going to do a whole lot more. They've allowed the time to get away from them, allowed complexities of life to take over; all the things that got in the way right in the midst of what was important to them and eliminated these big things from happening. If they hadn't stopped dreaming and had great structure in place, we wouldn't have those regretful conversations.

Susan: You're really highlighting the fact that we don't have placeholders for our dreams. We may secretly have dreams but we don't have a way of really ensuring they manifest.

Kort: We can even step back and talk about how dreams are not viewed as reality. Dreams in their infant stages look more like something that you want to attain like *Your Bigger Future*, but it's going to take change or several tools and resources that are not in your current reality in order to make it possible.

In order to achieve a big dream, you must be ready for a journey to a bigger future. It's not just the ending destination, it's a whole process. Some people are afraid to dream. They may feel it's childish to dream.

"You have all these dreams, John. Let's be honest, John, you work a 9 to 5 job, you have two kids and family. How could you possibly go to Italy for 2 weeks?"

The way society has been developed to where we are today, it's too traditional. In order to be normal, you have to have normal pursuits and normal dreams. We have to somewhat disrupt the normal way things look and say, "Yeah, you may feel a little insecure or a little bit scared, but not to worry, that's imagining real progress. You're going to go through this stage in order to get to *Your Bigger Future*," but they're just missing that support system.

There may be people that need to hear, "It's okay to pursue your dreams and to feel unsecure." They may need somebody to reassure them that in order to get to the end point, they're going to go through this phase of uncertainty.

For those who don't have a support system, where do you look for that support? How are you kept motivated? You don't have a mentor, your family, your mother, or your father is less than supportive, and you remember what you're up against, and slowly but surely the dream dies away. Without a support system, you are more likely to give up. You are left to rely on yourself. You may struggle and by doing that, you just settle on what is easy, never pushing yourself to achieve greatness. You stop working on creating *Your Bigger Future*, and your happiness is sacrificed.

Susan: People need to be given permission to dream again.

Kort: There needs to be a message to tell people it's okay to start dreaming again or better yet, it's okay to never stop chasing your dreams. If you don't dream it's like a slow death. I know that's aggressive but we see it every day and it's real. You may have hit your pinnacle, the climax of your launch angle of where you're headed with your future. If that high moment is in the past, wow, you may not have the same energy, drive, passion for life that you had before. **Ask yourself, what are you living for now?**

Susan: What role do you think fear of failure plays in this, Kort? If I actually put my dream out to the world and I don't reach it, will I feel worse than if I never tried for my dream at all?

Kort: People don't like to lose. People don't like to fail, and the fear of failure for some might be greater than the drive to accomplish the dream, which is very natural. But what are the dynamics to combat that fear? If this is something you struggle with, I believe you need to examine your lack of confidence more closely. It goes back to having the tools, resources and most importantly the support in order to make your dreams possible. All these play a big role in creating confidence and completing more big dreams.

Dreams and goals don't happen just by the snap of a finger. Big dreams take a tremendous amount of dedication and hard work. I do think people are scared of failure. To sacrifice all that time and hard work could be devastating for them to fail. "Everybody else is succeeding in their smaller future, why can I just settle here?"

SUCCESS-O-METER

"If I go for a bigger future, then I could fail at that bigger future and what are they going to say? 'See, that's why you don't go after dreams like that. Stay right over here where everybody's normal, and we'll all be successful together in this small but comfortable life.'" That's my perception of how I see things with some of the people we have met with all over the world.

"If you can dream it, you can do it."

Walt Disney

How Dreams Can Change Your View Of What Is Possible...

Susan: Can you articulate some examples of the types of dreams you're talking about for someone who doesn't quite have their arms around what some of the things they could or should be dreaming about?

Kort: Sure! First, they are really big and span across all aspects of your life. I'm very passionate about golf. One of my dreams is to play the top 100 golf courses in the US, and then I want to play the top 100 golf courses in the world. Somebody actually said to me "Oh Kort, you should not chase that dream. I've already tried to do it myself, and it's impossible. I mean, you might as well save yourself the time. Why would you do it?"

I looked them right in the face and said, "I happen to know two people, one who has played 87 of them and one who has done all 100, and one is in their mid-forties, and the other one is in their early fifties. They've done it so why can't I? Why can't anyone?"

We all have the abundance of relationships, time, and money to pursue whatever future we desire. This is America! Anything is possible here.

I'm guessing the person who tried to talk me out of going for my dream has never met somebody who accomplished this much progress toward this dream or one like it, or they wouldn't be so quick to try and talk me out of it. Having role models plays a bigger role than imagined when it comes to reaching for your dreams. **You have to believe you have what it takes to achieve your dreams.**

Another example recently happened with a nurse who is close to retirement. Actually this nurse is a big part of the reason why I have so much passion for writing this book. She's one of my clients, part of a corporate group I work with, and she is one of the best savers among all of our retirement plan clients. I've been meeting with her for roughly four or five years. In the last year I met with her, I mentioned, "After looking at your accounts it looks like you're going to retire securely."

She challenged me about this. "No. That can't be possible. Run those numbers again." I ran them again and again, and I showed her at the pace she was saving if she retired in the next two to three years, she would have enough money in her retirement account to replace her entire nursing income.

She pushed back from the table and was quiet for a minute. Then she said, "Wow! I'm really going to reach this!" I said, "Oh yeah. In fact you'd be hard pressed to screw it up."

She made somewhere around $50,000-$55,000 a year and she was saving 22% of her income as of this last year. She's on track to do it. I said to her, "Now this is a reality, what are you going to do in your retirement? How are you going to spend your day?" She was quiet again for another 15 or 20 seconds. Finally she said, "I'm not sure."

I told her "I'll be back in six months. When I get back, I'd love to hear what new dreams you have. And now that you're this close to accomplishing your dream of retiring what are you going to do with that freedom?"

Sure enough, I showed up, saw her again and said, "Have you given any thought to those dreams?" She said, "Yeah. You know, I'm still not sure that retirement is going to happen." I told her "It's a fact. It's not debatable. So, what are you going to do with your life?" She said, "I'm Italian, and I would love more than anything in the world to spend seven to ten days in Italy going to cooking classes." She goes on to say, "I have to tell you something. I hadn't even thought about what my dreams were. I'd been so focused on making sure I could retire that I didn't even think about my years in retirement.

There are other people in her same group who are not saving as much. Retirement is not as important to them, but they're focused on completing other dreams now. They know how much she is saving; it's common knowledge. They know what the recipe is in order to make it happen. They're just scared to take the risk she has, and once they find out that she's now going to spend her retirement, going to Italy every year to take cooking classes, it'll filter back into the group. I believe that's what's about to happen. She's mere months away from all this becoming a reality. The lists of types of dreams are endless across all categories of her life. I believe after knocking off a few of her first few dreams she won't stop there.

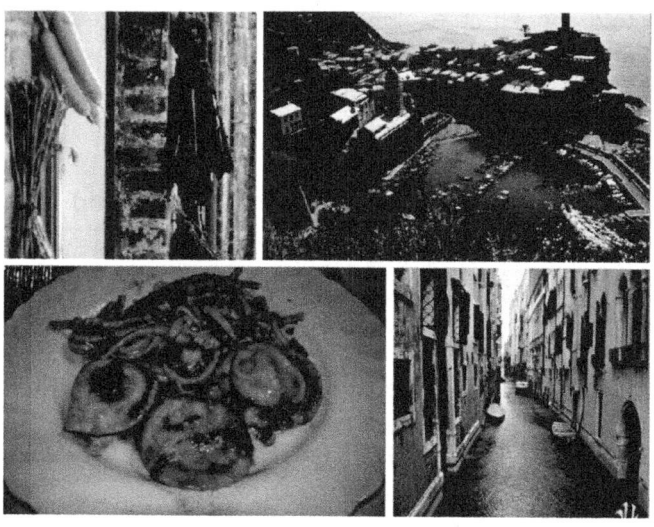

Susan: Italy! That's exciting. I can see where this is very life changing. It's getting to the root of why we get up every day and make a living! I hope it's not just to pay the mortgage and eat. There's got to be more to life than that, right?

Kort: I asked her, "Are you going to go alone?" She

smiled again. She's a widow and she wanted to find love again. She said, "I hope I'm able to find enough free time to meet somebody with whom I can share these moments."

Dreams are very sensitive, very emotional and very personal. There is so much about the emotion and feelings behind a dream; there's a vulnerable nature to them. It took me asking her a couple of times about what her new dreams were and a lot of thought on her part to get to the point where she was able to share a really big dream of hers.

She actually dreamed about going to Italy, but I don't know if she would have reached that point of realization if she never had shared any of it or felt the comfort to be open up about her dreams. I don't know if she would have gotten to that point if she hadn't been asked what her big dream was. See, it's the dreaming that allows the bigger future to unfold.

" Twenty years from now you will be more disappointed by the things you didn't do than by the ones you did. So throw off the bowlines. Sail away from the safe harbor. Catch the trade winds in your sails. Explore. Dream. Discover. "

Mark Twain

How To Use Dreams To Create Your Bigger Future...

Susan: What do you mean by a bigger future Kort?

Kort: There's another great book called The Dream Manager. It breaks dreams into twelve different categories or classes: physical, emotional, spiritual, intellectual, psychological, material, professional, financial, creative, adventure, legacy and character.

The Dream Manager 12 Categories Of Dreams

PHYSICAL	EMOTIONAL	INTELLECTUAL	SPIRITUAL
PSYCHOLOGICAL	MATERIAL	PROFESSIONAL	FINANCIAL
CREATIVE	ADVENTURE	LEGACY	CHARACTER

All these different areas or categories in your life where your dreams may lie provide a foundation for *Your Bigger Future*. These categories are relatively all encompassing and everything that somebody may dream is their future and would coincide with one of the categories. If you had a dream you were working towards for each category, it would provide a higher level of fulfillment. If you intend to pursue your dreams and create a bigger future, each of your dreams could be broken down into one of the categories. It's all very personal. Some people may have more material dreams than others, while other may have more intellectual dreams. Dreams can be creative, adventurous, or even professional. They should really stretch you.

In order to achieve *Your Bigger Future* you have to evaluate your dreams. Each person has to look at what's important to them and take inventory in these categories and say, "Okay, what are my dreams in this area?" Document those dreams. I can't stress that enough. Write them down!

Document...document...document. **Write 10 dreams. Then write 20, then write 50, then write 100, and save all the dreams you have.** Don't do any censoring at this point. Have them in one place, so you can see your dreams and understand how they're going to fulfill your life. Then you can look at them and figure out who's going to be a part of them? How much is that dream going to cost? How long is it going to take in order to reach it? Are there check points?

In order to create *Your Bigger Future*, you have to look at what your dreams are and then break them down into what steps you can take in order to get there. Who needs to be involved? Share your dreams with the people who want you to be successful and make them part of your support group. What resources will you need? Will there be advice you're going to need? Do you need mentors to accomplish this dream? Do you need to talk to people who have accomplished this dream before? Is this something that nobody's accomplished before? Is this something that's so unique that it's never been done? Don't get discouraged if you don't know the answers to all these questions right from the start. All of this is a process.

This reminds me of one of our dreamers who has a phenomenal support team. Chris's dream was to rebuild his dream car, which happens to be his father Al's old corvette. Together, the two of them tackled this dream and had a great time doing it. It took years and he had the support from his wife, Katie, which would allow him to escape for a few hours at a time.

This dream had the right players involved and allowed for him to achieve this awesome experience with his father. His new dream is to pass this car down to his son, Ross, meaning this car would have three generations in the driver's seat! Their passion will live on!

It is building the framework of what a bigger future looks like for YOU. I don't think dreams are the same for any one person in America or the world today. Sure there will be some crossover, but not all 100 dreams. After all, no one is exactly like you, so your dreams will be unique as well. I believe you have to figure out what is important to you with your core values and what you want your future to look like. Put a supportive environment in place full of people who want to complete your dreams with you and/or want you to achieve all of your dreams. Revisit your dreams with them as often as you possibly can and make sure that you're securing the course to success.

Reaching your dreams and building *Your Bigger Future* is never a destination. We know a bigger future is a journey, so no matter how small it seems, it is building progress. It's working towards something, accomplishing a goal along the path to a big dream this week, this month, this quarter, this year, and beyond. Pretty soon, you've created a bigger future by adding all these things up.

That's how I look at it, and that's how I recommend everyone go about building their bigger future as well.

Susan: I want to highlight a few things you pointed out. If you haven't been dreaming your whole life for any of the number of reasons we mentioned earlier, dreaming and building a bigger future may not be something that comes naturally.

It's almost like they need to build up their dreaming muscle. At first, their dreams may start out pretty small, testing the waters. But success breeds success, so over time they may get bigger and bolder.

Kort: I can remember back to that conversation in particular with my nurse client. She was giggling like a little kid. She's like, "Do you know how great it would be?" Then, she was laughing. She could see herself in the class over in Italy. She was smiling the whole time she was describing it to me. Her face was radiant. It was very emotional and lots of senses were going crazy. That look on her face was like, "Oh, I can be a kid again! Now you're telling me I have permission to be a dreamer. "

She had this throwback moment, this giggle. For a minute, why would I ever challenge the way she was laughing and processing the information because she had done something she hadn't given herself permission to do? For 30 years, she hadn't really dreamed and thought it was ok. She just reacted to whatever she needed to accomplish in that moment and had done it over and over and over again but, you know what, it created success for her and has now given her the ability to start dreaming again.

Susan: Agreed! It's so key. You are giving people permission to start dreaming again, and I love what you said about sharing the dream. Don't keep your dreams locked up inside of you. Having the dream isn't enough. The laundry needs to get done, and your grandmother's sick, and your mom needs to go to the doctor. There's a lot of stuff going on in life. Dreams easily get pushed to the back because something more pressing is vying for your attention. That's why it's so important to share your dreams and enroll others in the process.

Pipe Dream | **Bigger Dream**

Kort: Creating accountability is just as important as the dream itself. If you only have the dream and don't have any structure for making it happen, we call those pipe dreams. We leave it to fate whether or not it ever happens. But if you surround yourself with the support group who will help hold you accountable to your dreams and don't want to see you fail, then there are no big dreams completely out of reach. That's not leaving it to chance. Once you make the giant leap and become committed to this dream, then it's almost like going away from this smaller future you were headed towards. You don't want to fail, so you don't want to even begin to do it. However once you've made the leap and said, "I'm going to go and pursue this dream," and you've created a support group who has knowledge of what you're doing, they're going to keep you accountable and the last thing you want to do is fail. Nobody wants to fail.

The accountability is critical for your own success, adding positive reinforcement is certainly the added pressure needed to succeed. Also the people that you love and love you are going to be so excited when they learn how many exciting dreams you have planned together.

"When we are motivated by goals that have deep meaning, by dreams that need completion, by pure love that needs expressing, then we truly live life."

Greg Anderson

Don't Focus on Goals, Focus on Dreams...

Susan: Can you make a distinction for us between a goal and a dream?

Kort: Dreams are bigger than goals. If my dream is to be extremely fit and have great health, then my goal is to run 20 minutes a day, six days a week for that period of time. **So goals are used to accomplish dreams.**

A dream is, in my opinion, a bigger destination than a goal because you need to stack up your goals in order to reach a bigger dream. People often create goals every year. They create a New Year's resolution, but I want someone's dream to be much bigger than that! Dreams, in reality, are bigger future items.

What's your dream job? You're not going to get to your dream job in one day; it could take you a couple of years. My goal now is to read 10 self-help books, or 10 books around a category that's going to serve my bigger future which is being prepared in order to get the dream job of my life.

See the distinction? The goals fuel the dream, but the dream is the bigger landscape and vision that pulls you forward and keeps you motivated.

A perfect example of goals and dreams can be taken from a couple more dreamers at Penrose Brewing Company. Eric and Tom had a dream to open up a brewery out in the western suburbs of Chicago. It was a quite a journey to get to the first brew date but they celebrated every goal and milestone along the way to accomplishing their big dream. The dream doesn't stop there as they are constantly introducing new beers each month that inspired them to go down this path in the first place. They have a lot to celebrate now that the world gets to enjoy their beer!

Reading self-help books may not be enough motivation for you, but each day focusing little by little on making progress toward that dream job and all of a sudden this big dream doesn't look so daunting.

Maybe your dream is to graduate with a great computer science and coding background, so I can be a developer who creates web applications someday. In order to do that, a lot of smaller goals need to be achieved to make that a reality. I look at goals as stepping stones or nice milestones. They may be day by day, they may be week by week, month by month, but dreams are big. Dreams are those things that seem scary, they may even seem out of reach but the dream will just absolutely keep you alive.

Goals are more task-like, but they're destinations, too. They're the shorter milestones along the way.

" Dream lofty dreams, and as you dream, so shall you become. Your vision is the promise of what you shall one day be; your ideal is the prophecy of what you shall at last unveil."

James Allen

Why You Should Dream Big!

Susan: Very well said. It's funny when you were sharing that. It's almost like you want your dream to be big enough almost to take your breath away, right? It's almost like, "Oh my, I don't know. I shouldn't really have that big of a dream should I?" You're saying actually, that's the right one, the one that almost scares you. Pick that dream.

Kort: Yes I would say so. There are a lot of people that would say, "Yeah, I have dreams." They may document them and one person would say, "Oh yeah, I have to say those are just goals. Those don't look like dreams to me." We need to extend those a little further, and then you'll have yourself some dreams, but they wouldn't know that without a support group. Somebody who has some challenging recommendations against what they're doing.

The gauge between goals and dreams are all relative to someone's current position, but no matter your position it should definitely take your breath away. It should be something you go, "Woo! That might take a lifetime." Or, it may take relationships, resources, some advice, and connections to the right people. You might have that in a few years, but nobody knows that for certain when they begin the pursuit.

Susan: It strikes me how important what you're sharing is, Kort, because no one else is teaching us how to dream again. Here we are in 2014, and a lot of people live like kings and queens used to live. In fact, a lot of broke people live better than kings and queens of old.

With our big screen TVs, our iPhones, iPads, movies, clean water, access to healthcare, when you boil it down for the most part life is pretty amazing. By historical standards anyway, our lives here in North America are pretty good even when they are not. Not everyone will recognize or even agree with this, but life isn't horrible for a lot of people. And so in a way, that may be getting in our way of dreaming. We aren't unhappy enough you know?

Kort: Yeah, I think you're right. There's a lot of people who are able to live in ways that they never could have years ago, but what if we said to ourselves in 50 years, what will the American dream look like, or what will be people's dream life then? Will it be the same as it was 50 years ago or it is today?

We probably could agree that it's going to be different. It's not going to be the same. Nothing ever stays the same, it seems like. If we know that life is pretty good, what about 50 years ago or even 75 years ago? Did they think that they were not living the dream then?

What did their bigger future look like? Did they feel like everybody was living pretty well then? I would say yes. There's probably a little bit larger disparity. We've had a government that just intervenes and says we need to level this out a little bit more and give people a better standard of living. They had the ability to use credit devices versus only being able to do it by cash, and if you didn't have cash you couldn't accomplish it. The use of credit has allowed for the level of risk to go up. A majority of people are now using credit financing to buy their dream house today. You couldn't do that back in the day, so more dreams are happening now.

I would, without question, challenge the fact that in 50 years, dreams will be even bigger than they are today. How we go about achieving them may change, but the dreaming should still come into play for creating a bigger future. In fact, there are now companies that are working on giving people rides to the moon and back. We weren't talking about that 50 years ago. We weren't talking about iPods, iPads, or iPhones. Technology changes, and so do the dreams.

Susan: You're absolutely right. The question remains, **if on your deathbed you looked back at your life, are you going to be okay with what you've done and what you've accomplished? If the answer is no, it's time to get dreaming again.**

Kort: If you were to ask a large percentage of the world as you walked up to them individually and looked them in the eye, "Tell me, are you living your dream?" They'll look at you like, "What? What are you talking about?" I would say, "No. The life you have, did you dream of this? Ten years ago, did you think that you'd be living this life? Is this your dream life?"

We had a dreamer that reached a point in his career and realized, "I am not doing what I thought I would be doing." After some thought, Matt came to the conclusion it was time to go back and get his MBA degree. Since graduating he has seen the advantages of going after the life he wanted. It turns out that he wanted a combination of his previous career and a new real estate focus, but with a different twist that his MBA allowed him to make a reality.

They would look at you, and after exchanging a few awkward looks back and forth, and then eventually they would give you the honest truth and they would say, "No," because you know what? If they were living their dreams, you wouldn't have to ask them. They would be radiating it.

People who are living their dreams, in my experience, you never need to be asked if they are living their dreams. They're radiating it so much that you want to absorb it because you're going to say, "Man, this person has got it." You never have to ask the question. It's a non-verbal. They have this aura.

A great example of this would be another one of our dreamers, Paul, who started taking Second City improvisation classes to tackle his fear of speaking in front of his peers. What started with one class turned into several classes, and eventually spilled over into his lifestyle and an improved career path! His confidence went through the roof and those closest to him could tell the moment he went on stage at the end of his program. His world had changed by achieving just one dream. He picked up that aura.

That does not always mean that they're financially successful. They could have any occupation. They could be a social worker. They could be a teacher. They could have a job that does not compensate highly or one that does, but they dreamed of doing this their whole life. They could be a fireman. They could be a police officer. They could be an investment banker. No matter the career choice, they're extremely passionate about what they're doing. They're fulfilled with the world that they've created, and they're exuding that.

It's an attitude. It's a passion. It is not always monetary. It's more of a sense of internal fulfillment. It's not just inside of them because it is now spewing out. It's coming out of their body, and they create an environment around them that makes people want to be around them. People want to engage with them because the dream level that they're operating at is inspiring. The world that they have created is the result of them living for their dreams. They are setting goals to facilitate those dreams of theirs, for so long, and pushing so hard that it has become almost like a force field. You come into it, and you can feel the energy and power they have.

Whatever they're at, they're the best of their trade, or they certainly are pushing to be the best in their trade, and it's infectious. It really is. When I'm around those people, I feel like I have the best conversations.

I had that conversation this morning with an author. He's been uber successful but it wasn't because he started writing books or because of his last engagement. He was successful long ago. It just looks like now is the destination. I would have bet that there wouldn't be a whole lot of difference between him when he began pursuing his dream career and now. It just looks a little different, but I would think because of some material things that are in there, in general, their attitude, their drive, their passion, everything that comes with them, you just say, "Well, this person is almost larger than life because they have so much energy and excitement about the life that they're living."

Susan: What you're saying is, when you land on the dream and are going for it, there's a vibrancy, there's a liveliness, there's an enthusiasm, if you will, that you may not have if you're just going through the motions and showing up for work and doing your job and going home. There isn't as much excitement when you're just going through life without a dream.

Kort: Find the five things that are most important to somebody who fits that description of what we're talking about, and ask them if you can take these five items away. Have them describe what it would do to them.

They probably will have the worst look on their face because you'd be taking away items that they spent a lifetime building, right? Will that be their career, their family, their faith that they have in God, a hobby that they have, or a vacation home?

What Are The Top 5 Most Important Things In Your Life?

What If One Was Taken Away?

Whatever those big dreams are, if you take those things away, they've been working their tail off for them, and it has probably put that attitude into them saying, "Hey, I've accomplished some of these," and they're doing more of them as we speak.

It's funny I brought up this conversation I had today with an author. I thought he had just written one book. Boy was I wrong. I asked him, "Is this your first project, your first book?" He said, "Oh, no, I've written these three books here, and I'm really excited about this new one I'm working on."

The point is that he's never going to stop. He's never going to stop doing this. This is his passion, and he wants to be really great at it. He's met the bestselling authors; he made it a point to integrate with them. He said, "Pretty soon, I'll become one of them." I said, "Who?" He said, "These people who are really great at this."

He just knew it. He had that confidence. He knew what was going to occur. He knew his dream of being at that level of the best authors was coming true. I didn't get a chance to really get into the reason and ask, "Why are you doing this?" He knows why he's doing this. He knows it's his purpose, and he radiates that energy in his conversations. He is not just going through the motions.

His dream is to be a great author and publish more books because that is his purpose, and he knows why he's supposed to do these. People need help with these things, so he's giving them material to get them to pursue their dreams, like me writing this book on this very subject.

"Dreams are renewable. No matter what our age or condition, there are still untapped possibilities within us and new beauty waiting to be born."

Dr. Dale E. Turner

Why You Should Never Stop Dreaming...

Susan: Can you start too late Kort? Is there a time when it's like, "Oh, you missed the boat. You should've been dreaming 30 years ago?" Is there an age limit on dreams?

Kort: Age limit? No. Zero age limit. I probably shouldn't use this as an example, but I laughed because I was watching America's Got Talent the other night, (never watched the show in my life), and a 74 year old man goes on there, singing, and the place went absolutely nuts! He nailed it. They said, "Why didn't we discover you earlier?" He said, "I was trying to build my retirement as a bartender." They said, "Were you successful?" He said, "Yeah. I retired. I got my income put away, and I started doing what I loved which is singing." all at age 74.

I'm sure that will turn into a success story, and I don't know the whole background piece on it, but I believe you can point out multiple scenarios of people who just never stopped dreaming, right?

My grandfather is one of the biggest dreamers I have met. He recently passed away at age 88, and he was still taking design classes at Arizona State University the year he passed away. He was actively involved in several big dreams he had. He was tired of all the forest fires that were occurring all over the western US, and his dream was to put a stop to all these fires having such devastating effects on peoples' lives and their homes. He envisioned a system that houses could have installed where if a fire was coming, a heat sensor would go off and it would essentially soak the house, but would prevent it from being a total loss. He was 88, and he was still going strong. He was still dreaming.

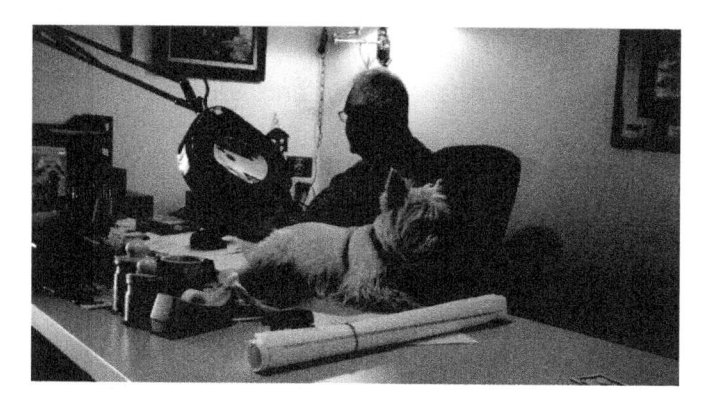

Dreaming is ageless. It should be. There should be no end to this. You should never stop dreaming. In fact, if you stop dreaming, it's over just like a horse going into retirement in the pasture. Your best days are over. If you are dreaming, you will live healthier longer. I really believe that. People who dream longer will live longer, and they will live better lives.

Susan: They'll certainly have a more enriching life.

Kort: Exactly.

> *"Dreams pass into the reality of action. From the action stems the dream again; and this interdependence produces the highest form of living."*

Anais Nin

Here's How the DreamNumber™ Online Application Works...

Susan: Tell us about your DreamNumber™ Web Application, Kort. Why did you create this?

Kort: We initially created our DreamNumber™ Web Application (www.Dream-Number.com) with the intention of solving the retirement calculation, helping people figure out how much money they will need to retire. But it has become a lot more than that. We do believe that part of creating a great foundation for *Your Bigger Future* is solving the retirement calculation because that is the core passion of ours, but life is so much more than just getting to retirement securely. We believe it all starts with the creation of a dream. The web application has the ability to help you manifest that dream. It begins with the categories that we mentioned earlier. The system has the ability to create custom dreams outside the scope of even what we've created. It's very robust.

We created a system and a platform where people can dream big and where they can go to get support for their dreams. As we talked earlier, it's very important to get the ongoing support to facilitate reaching your dreams.

The process of creating a dream through Dream-Number.com starts with creating an image for your dream. If your dream is to someday own a vacation home, most likely someone would have an image in their mind of what that might look like.

I believe every dream should have a customized look of what that dream is, so the person can see it, they can internalize an image. What that image does for them internally in order to see it and put them on a path to solving what's really important to them is one of the most critical steps. The image that belongs to that dream gives that dreamer the motivation. That one image is important to them; they want that image to be their reality.

It could be anything from travel, to personal hobbies, to education or to professional pursuits... the list is endless. Then we attach a custom photo that represents that dream, and we describe in detail what the dream is. The web application walks you through all this: How much it's going to cost; how many other people are you sharing your dream with? The web application allows you to invite users to share the dream, so that they can be involved in your dream. We help you put a timeline around your dream. When is this dream going to occur? How long is it going to take for you to do this?

Then the system drills down further by asking if there's a financial element, it gives you an annual and a daily calculation on how much you would need to budget in order to make that a reality. A lot of our dreams have a financial element to them, but we need to know what that need is and how much we need to be saving to make this dream a reality.

The system provides you with a hub for all your dreams, all in one place. There's an email system which updates you and lets you know what your progression is with each dream. It allows you to allocate funds towards your dream. So when they allocate funds, they are directing savings from their banking or investment accounts directly towards their individual dreams. DreamNumber™ becomes a place to solve the focused savings necessary to make a dream a reality.

We've been doing some exercises where we create 100 dreams, customize them, and get the photos that go along with each dream. Then we post them out to the application and create benchmarks and then organize them and then figure out how you come back and monitor the progress you've made.

It's a very smooth process. We're continuing to improve it, but we feel great about where it's at today.

Susan: What you've done is create the framework for someone to manifest their dreams. Because of all the reasons we stated earlier where life gets in the way, this is a way to help keep your dream alive by being able to enroll others and by having a place where we can check in with our dreams and check progress on them. I love it.

Kort: There's a built in support element in there, too, so they can check in with us. We put our success stories on our blog, (blog.dream-number.com,) to keep people motivated and inspired. There are also interactions with social media.

We've been doing case studies where we're interviewing Dreamers and asking, "What's your dream? What big dreams have you been doing?" They share with us what they are dreaming about. We're talking about their success then enrolling them into Dream-Number.com and helping them use it as a hub. We are also determining how they're having success today in the way that they're doing things and then figuring out how Dream-Number.com can be a facilitator to improving the way that they're doing this. They have some other bigger dreams that they haven't pursued yet that they can put in motion and use the system in order to accomplish that.

We have a couple that is not afraid of the hard work that goes into pursuing their bigger dreams. Steve and Katie were hit pretty hard with the housing market crash, but they supported each other, worked really hard and saved enough to purchase their dream home for their family. Now DreamNumber™ assists them with expanding their family, education for their children and volunteering. They love how they are able to track their progress to their dreams in their Dream Profile. It keeps them motivated!

Susan: I can imagine seeing other people tracking their progress on their goals and dreams may inspire you to go for a bigger dream. Some of us may start off dreaming too small, but when we see other people striving for even bigger things, it may give us permission to reach even further. This will give you a supportive environment for reaching even bigger.

Kort: Where is a safe place for us to dream today? Where it's not just acceptable...it's encouraged! Where it's the norm! Where can we do that?

That's what was behind Dream-Number.com. It's a safe environment to dream bigger, where you can build *Your Bigger Future*. Other people can't see your dreams, unless you choose to share them with other Dreamers.

Everyone's a little different. Some people want to share. Others don't. Some want to show how they lost a lot of weight. It was a dream of mine to get back into my high school jeans, and now I want to talk about how I did it. That environment needs to exist in the world. There needs to be a place where it's okay to dream. It can be private or public, and the platform is like a dream accelerator for you.

Most of what we're seeing is very few dreams are accomplished by people doing it by themselves. Very little of it is "I'm doing this dream, and I only want to do it by myself. I don't want to do it with anybody else." We don't hear people saying that.

In fact, most of the dreams in order for them to be accomplished have to have other people involved. Very few people ever reach their dreams and say "I accomplished this. I did it 100% on my own. There was nobody else involved. I didn't use any tools or resources, just my bare hands. This is all me."

We're seeing people who have a strong network of support and have probably dreamed about the people they wanted involved in order to achieve these big dreams and create this life that they had.

In fact, that has become a huge theme across the

board. We're seeing a lot of integration on the blog, and that tells us that people like the community nature and love the safe environment where it's okay to dream big over here and to be able to say the five of us went on this dream vacation together, and this is how we did it.

Susan: I would imagine for your 100 golf courses dream you don't want to go golf by yourself.

Kort: Exactly. You don't play a foursome by yourself. In fact, I played one of my dream courses by myself, and I swore to myself I would never do it again. I may have knocked this one off, but I won't do any more by myself. It doesn't have the same meaning. I might be checking one off the list, but when I went to take that photo on the course, where are my three buddies? Where's my family who is supposed to be there hanging with me at the same time?

Susan: Not the same thing.

Kort: Once I started sharing that dream with other people, they started saying, "Hey, if you're going to any of these courses, you tell me." Because they want to be involved in the dream, so there's a whole community element. "Don't leave me out of your dreams because I share that dream with you! That's a dream of mine, too. Because you're making this a reality, it can be a reality for me, too. If you're going to go, call me." People want to help you reach your dreams and celebrate with you!

Susan: It's an enrollment process and a support structure for you. You get other people involved who maybe never thought to have a dream that big. They didn't think it was possible, but they start seeing you achieving your dreams, and you enroll them in your dream which then may become a part of their dream. I love it.

Kort: We had a beautiful couple, Jason and Victoria, who were planning an amazing destination wedding in Turks and Caicos. It was a very emotional story. Victoria tragically lost both her parents in the nine months leading up to the wedding. Her dream of having her fairy tale wedding surrounded by all her family and friends suddenly changed.

After the wedding, we went through everything with her, and I said, "How would you use DreamNumber™? She's said, "If you could give me access to people who've taken these dream vacations, even beyond this wedding that was so emotional, I would use it because I want to be able to interact with them about how they did it."

I showed her the travel dreams on the website, but she said that she not only dreams of her travels. She has other things that were big dreams of hers as well. Victoria wanted to be able to share with other people, or pick their brain about how they were planning their big dreams. There's almost this community element of meeting people and creating a social network in a sense, a social environment for them to exchange detailed information about dreams.

Susan: I really hope, Kort, that this is the start of a movement. We are just not getting this message anywhere else in life. It's just not being taught like you are talking about it here.

Kort: It comes back to, what are your dreams? What does *Your Bigger Future* look like? What do you want in life because not everybody wants the same thing?

To be honest with you, this message isn't getting out to people, and it bothers me.

The reality is that some people will catch the message, some people won't catch it until later, and then there may be some people who never catch it. There's no doubt that this message needs to go on. I need it personally for my dreams. I needed it so bad that I started doing it myself and giving it to other people. That's how bad it was because there was nobody else who was giving it to me.

When you realize that nobody else is supporting your dream that is when you need to change what's occurring. I saw that in my career; I saw that in my life. I said, "I have nobody who's involved at the level that I need them to be." I started doing it on my own, which is a little unique I guess. Some people probably do that, too. It's probably not totally unique. I'm sure some people do it.

This message needs to get out there. It needs to be in schools. It needs to be wherever people are on the rise, before their energy falls off, to catch the wave, if you will, and just continue to ride that thing all the way in. Rather than some people getting to a point where they're starting to diminish, do we say it's too late? No. We may be able to turn them, but let's catch them before they go in the wrong direction.

We would probably be a little bit naïve to think that we'd get everybody thinking this way, but if we can influence one then two then ten and then a hundred then a thousand, I'm ready to do it, and I'm ready to do it now and I'm ready to get this message out. Keep dreaming people!

I learned a long time ago there are probably some ways to influence a larger sum and this, with the book and with the message, I believe is probably the fastest and most impactful way. Beyond that is what I thought I was doing from a retirement planning standpoint, but it wasn't large enough. The future that I needed to serve needed to be bigger because I wanted it to really have enough impact, and retirement wasn't important to everybody, and some people dream in different areas.

Hello
my name is
Dream Consultant

The way I look at it today is that I'm a Dream Consultant and not really a Retirement Planner or Retirement Consultant. Retirement might be one of the things we talk about, but in reality we are talking about a lot of other things. We can set up an account and do whatever we wanted to do, but let's talk about these dreams. Let's get those on paper. Let's get those into the application Dream-Number.com, and let's get started on making these things a reality.

I am extremely passionate about this, and I don't think it will diminish. I believe it's only going to grow because we're in the infant stages of this movement. We're in a very good position because it's not a message that's gone on and on, and to know that there are people who are receptive to it means that we just need to find more of those people.

Susan: Yeah. It's an inspiring message, and I love that you aren't assuming most people have similar goals. Not everyone wants to end up in retirement with a pile of money at retirement because there are probably a lot of other dreams that are being missed out on along the way. How can we make sure that those happen as well?

Kort: If you look up the definition of 'retirement' in the dictionary, it means to be 'put out of use'. Before we were helping people get prepared to be put out of use, I don't know how helpful that was. Retirement means something different to everybody.

Even bigger than that is leading up to retirement, what are their dreams today? To be honest, some people never dream of retiring, meaning, they never dreamed of being put out of use. If you're never going to be put out of use, and you're always going to be useful, what are you going to do while you're useful?

It's never too late to dream, so you create a lifestyle that you can live forever. For years retirement has taken on this connotation that it means to be successful. He retired, so he was a person who was successful. I don't think that's the case any longer. Nowadays I don't think every person has to retire because not everybody needs or wants to be put out of use.

I believe you need to create an environment where you can do what you want, do what you love, and you'll always be happy, fulfilled and live the longest life that you're supposed to live.

That's a lot more impactful, and we are serving a much larger purpose if we can help people accomplish that versus some retirement calculation only to then be put out of use and have more money, pass it on to somebody else who won't have the same purpose, the same intention for it as they had before that.

Susan: You are giving us permission to say, "Whoa! What are you passionate about? What do you want to do with yourself?" and giving us permission to go and dream that now. It may take some planning. It's going to take some action as you said. It's going to take some sacrifice along the way to get there, but without the dream, you just show up at the end, look around and ask, "Is this it?"

Thank you for sharing with us Kort! Truly inspiring! If someone has a question, how can they get in touch with you?

Kort: They can reach us at info@dream-number.com, or they can call our office at 866-299-9944, extension 1002. You'll be put in touch with the DreamNumber™ team in our office here, or you can check us out at www.dream-number.com, or like I mentioned, go to our blog at blog.dream-number.com. We're definitely on all the social media sites as well.

Susan: Any final thoughts here Kort?

Kort: The most important thing is to start dreaming and write those dreams down. Start now! 10…20…50…100…etc. Go to www.dream-number.com and start to put those dreams into motion. Write them down, customize them, apply inspirational pictures, create goal dates and start to get the momentum going there. By writing your dreams down, you've made it real. Then share those dreams with other people that are going to be involved. Create accountability. Add dates. Create a time line. Add the financials, you know what it costs, and begin reviewing them.

The people that are a part of these dreams need to be reviewing them with you and making them a reality. The fulfillment of completing one, two, three, four, five is just going to build and build and happiness will go up, confidence will go up, and everything will become clear. **You can do this!**

In fact, that first one might not even be a dream. It might have been a goal. Pretty soon, that the momentum will begin to take over, and the success pattern will become repeatable, and I believe we're going to go back to those infant days in our lives when we were dreaming all the time, and mom and dad said, "Little Johnny, you know, I'm really proud of you that this is your dream. You know what? We're going to do that." They gave and equipped him with the tools, resources and advice, whatever he needed in order to make it real. I believe we're going to get back there and that would be a bigger future for all of us.

Hopefully, a large majority of America catches the wave and becomes a part of this movement. We want that to happen. The world will become a much better place.

I leave you with the inspiration and the permission and the confidence to say this is a world that we need to operate in every day for the rest of our lives. Not until retirement, not during retirement, not up to it, now; not, tomorrow; not, the day after. It's an everyday thing. It needs to be your lifestyle. It is how life needs to look, and society will become a much better place for us all. Starting dreaming...NOW!

Notes & Key Insights

" The future belongs to those who believe in the beauty of their dreams. "

Eleanor Roosevelt

Here's Exactly How to Get Started on *Your Bigger Future* Today...

You already know that life can get busy at times and in the way of your best intentions. The challenging part is creating a supportive environment to help you manifest your dreams.

That is where we come in. We help people just like you establish the support system and road map need to make your dreams a reality!

Step 1: Start by writing down first 10, then 20, then 50, then 100 dreams! It is that easy!

Step 2: Sign up for a **FREE** trial account today at **www.Dream-Number.com** and start building, budgeting and executing your dreams today!

Step 3: Share your dreams with your support group, whether it be family, friends, mentors, or centers of influence. These are the people you are going to be completing your dreams with. They will keep you accountable!

Step 4: We take it from here. Take a minute to visit our blog at **blog.dream-number.com** for inspiring and exciting stories from other dreamers like yourself!

Most people give up on their dreams way too soon or stop dreaming all together. Now you can get all of the support you need to keep the momentum going to achieve your dreams.

If you would like help on your journey, email us at **info@YourBiggerFuture.com**.

"Go confidently in the direction of your dreams. Live the life you've imagined."

Henry David Thoreau

Epilogue

Have you pictured what *Your Bigger Future* is going look like after accomplishing at least one of your great big dreams? I already know that your life will be changed in the best possible way. By achieving just one dream, you will notice:

- **Your confidence increasing.**

- **Your life feeling more fulfilled.**

- **You will develop a thirst for life and everything that it has to offer.**

- **You will notice your family and friends turning to you for inspiration and motivation.**

- **You will develop a drive to complete larger dreams.**

- **You will develop an addiction for success.**

I said it once, and I will say it again, the likelihood of achieving your dream increases when you write it down. We are simply providing you the opportunity to write down your dreams and increase the likelihood of achieving your dreams.

Don't let *Your Bigger Future* slip away, start achieving your dreams today.

Explore the Official DreamNumber™ Website

www.dream-number.com

Visit The Site To Do Any Of The Following:

- Complete the *Your Bigger Future's* interview. Then interview your friends, family and colleagues.

- Download and print *Your Bigger Future's* Organizer.

- Download and print the four strategies on achieving *Your Bigger Future.*

- Sign up for your FREE trial of DreamNumber ™.

- Connect with a Dream Consultant and learn how to achieve *Your Bigger Future* with DreamNumber™.

- Connect with other Dreamers to celebrate your achievements and *Your Bigger Future.*

- Share strategies and stories with others through our blog (blog.dream-number.com) and social media.

Your Bigger Future **Interview Questions**

- What were your dream(s) as a kid? What are you dream(s) today?

- Do you feel as if you're living your dream(s) now?

- What drives you every day?

- Why do you do what you do? How much satisfaction has this created in your life?

- What has gone into these decisions to chase your dream(s)?

- Who was your biggest supporter/motivator and what did they do that helped you the most?

- What was the first step you took towards achieving your dream?

- What financial steps did you go through to work toward this dream? How long have you been planning for this?

- How has your plan changed over the last 3 years? How do you think it will change in the next 3 years? Where do you think your dreams will be in 3 years?

- Would you have changed anything along the way to where you are today?

- Has the progress of your dream been a steady line or more of a rollercoaster?

- What are some of your wins along the way?

- What is your proudest moment to date?

- Do you feel you would work as hard as you do without this dream or others?

- What advice do you have for others pursuing their dreams?

- Could you imagine doing anything other than pursuing your dream?

The Four Strategies System For
Your Bigger Future

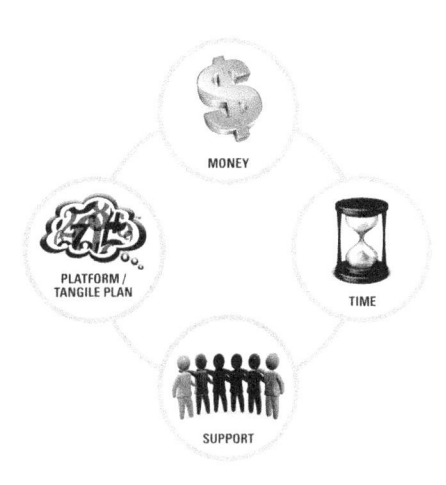

Strategy One: Time
Take 30 minutes to write down your dreams each week.

Strategy Two: Money
Understand the monetary needs Your Bigger Future will require and budget.

Strategy Three: Support
Share your dreams with your close circle, (family, friends and colleagues) and create a solid support system.

Strategy Four: Platform
Create a FREE trial of DreamNumber™ and start planning for Your Bigger Future.

We Want To Hear About *Your Bigger Future* Stories!

Your Bigger Future doesn't happen overnight, in fact, *Your Bigger Future* is a journey! We understand this journey, and want to celebrate the success you had with *Your Bigger Future* and using DreamNumber™.

We want to hear about this fantastic journey that you have taken. Tell us about your proudest moments! Tell us about your struggles and how you overcame them. Your story could be that extra support that someone else needs.

If you have a great story you want to share, please contact us at info@yourbiggerfuture.com! If you enjoyed this book, we would love to hear your thoughts, comments and ideas.

Share *Your Bigger Future* With Your Friends, Family And Colleagues

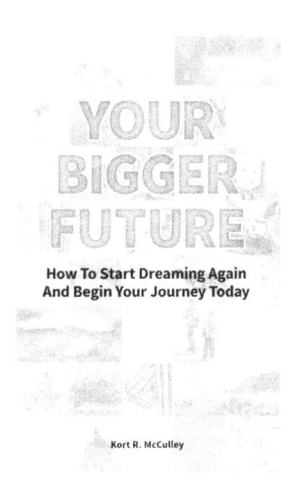

Your Bigger Future is available at online retailers or at www.yourbiggerfuture.com.

If you are interested purchasing *Your Bigger Future* in a large quantity, please contact us to discuss possible bulk discounts at info@yourbiggerfuture.com.

The group behind *Your Bigger Future* provides personal consultations, support and a platform for *Your Bigger Future*. For more information, please email us at info@yourbiggerfuture.com.

About The Author

Kort R. McCulley, AIF, MBA, is the Founder of Dream-Number.com, an online platform for helping you reach your dreams; Birdies For Cures, a 501(c)(3) charity focused on golf and raising money in the fight against cancer; and McCulley Financial Group, a Registered Investment Advisor in the State of Illinois. He holds various state insurance and securities licenses including the FINRA Series 7, 63, and 65, held through Triad Advisors. He has earned the Accredited Investment Fiduciary® (or AIF®) professional designation, awarded by the Center for Fiduciary Studies, which is associated with the University of Pittsburgh.

Kort has received formal training in investment fiduciary responsibility. He holds a Bachelor of Science in Economics and Finance from Western Illinois University then went on to complete his Masters of Business Administration (MBA) with an emphasis in Finance and International Business. He works closely with companies and individuals to help them pursue and accomplish their biggest dreams. His pursuit started with solving the retirement challenges people have but has since turned out to be a lot more than that.

Kort lives in Elmhurst, Illinois and when he's not working you can usually find him golfing, dining with friends, running, or participating in Bikram Yoga.